YOU

YOU

The Journey Begins

Dr Nirvadha Singh

Copyright © 2016 by Nirvadha Singh.

1st Edition   : February 2016
2nd Edition : June 2016

ISBN: Softcover   978-0-620-71621-5
               eBook   978-0-620-71622-2

All rights reserved. No part of this book may be used or reproduced by any means, graphic, electronic, or mechanical, including photocopying, recording, taping or by any information storage retrieval system without the written permission of the author except in the case of brief quotations embodied in critical articles and reviews.

Due to the dynamic nature of the internet, published links and web addresses may no longer be valid. All views expressed in this book reflect, solely, those of the author.

www.nirvadhasingh.com

SELF PUBLISHING SERVICES
www.blulotis.com

Contents

Chapter 1	:	You are your own best friend..................1
Chapter 2	:	Your past shapes your future. 9
Chapter 3	:	Faith and Fate.........................13
Chapter 4	:	Peace is a friendship which begins within you..............................17
Chapter 5	:	Fear, Failure and Doom; Replace your negative world into a positive life..........21
Chapter 6	:	Believe in 'You'.........................25
Chapter 7	:	The Healing Power of Love. 29
Chapter 8	:	You are your own competition. 33
Chapter 9	:	Be Yourself...............................37
Chapter 10	:	'You' are your greatest source of inspiration...............................41

I extend my gratitude to my family for their love and support provided as I had penned this book which I thus dedicate to them. Above all, my deepest faith in Our Creator for the wisdom provided which enables me to share this to our readers.

Chapter 1

You are your own best friend.

Dear Diary,

I have been distant from a very close friend. I haven't made enough time for this friendship. Having been so focused in other spheres of life, I completely ignored this special person who I am now trying to get in touch with before I fail to recognise this heart. I need to reach out to my most intimate friend, myself, my spirit, me.
The journey begins.

Yours truly,

Nirvadha

As I stand on the precipice of my thoughts, I realise that our Universe is vast and infinite however each individual views the world differently. These internal and external perceptions, attitudes and beliefs are what make 'You' as a complete person within the solar system. The key to the source of your being is how to view our dynamic world which has either a positive or negative influence upon you. Every experience from past to the present shapes your future.

When we experience negative scenarios, our thoughts become negative and this has a negative impact on our lives. The opposite holds true that when we experience positive incidences, we become motivated and feel happier. An example is if you have experienced a break-up in a relationship, you begin to feel as if you are not worthy. Your thoughts become dark and gloomy as you begin to doubt your own personality and thus become depressed. This depression results in a lack of sleep, loss of interest in your favourite hobbies and has an adverse impact on your physical well-being. Such is the power of negativity which can weigh you down like dead wood.

On the flip side of the coin, if you experience a positive incident such as receiving a compliment from your boss or loved one; you automatically feel elevated as the happy hormones and endorphins 'kick in'. You begin to feel as though you can conquer the world and usually everything runs smoothly that day. However, the big question is, how often do you remember the positive incidence as compared to the negative one? We are all guilty of being caught up in a cycle of remembering a negative incident much more often as compared to a positive one. *The first golden rule is being your own best friend.* Love yourself enough to think happy thoughts because if you always wish happiness unto others, why not wish the very same happiness unto yourself.

Every day is a brand new day and must be treated as a gift. There is room for improvement every second so grab that opportunity. If the day did not go well then do not wait for another day to start over when you can begin the very next second to create positive incidences to uplift your mood. *The second golden rule; as you think, you become the person defined by your thoughts.* Think happy thoughts, joyous thoughts and positive thoughts. Once you are able to undertake this you will be able to imbibe *the third golden rule; you are your own inspiration.* You have the power to heal yourself, heal your thoughts and uplift yourself.

Mind Map 1: How to heal yourself using your own healing powers.

Step 1 : Describe one negative incident in your lifetime.

_____

_____

_____

_____

Step 2 :   Now describe five positive incidences in your lifetime.

_____

_____

_____

_____

_____

Step 3 :   Next, list your strengths in the positive incidences above.

_____

_____

_____

_____

_____

_____

_____

_____

Step 4 :   Using step 3, approach step 1 to manage this negative incident

_____

_____

_____

_____

_____

Yes, you are on the right track. *The fourth golden rule; only you can find the solutions to your problems by focusing on your own strengths instead of your weaknesses.*

Having said the above which is all well and good but in life, I have experienced that regardless of how positive or negative one can be, you are always viewed upon your actions differently by different people. What is done in good faith by one person can be perceived as negative by another and vice versa. This is attributed to human behaviour and perceptions. It is how one views the world either through a peep hole or magnifying glass which is a reflection of their thought processes. *The fifth golden rule then manifests that it is not important how the world views you, but how 'You' view yourself.*

We tend to analyse other life forms, instances and circumstances but how often do we analyse ourselves? It is primary to reconnect with your inner self. By simple self-reflection, you can formulate an insight into your strengths and weaknesses. Using your strengths and weaknesses to your advantage, you can manipulate your day to that of a positive one regardless of the environment around you. Realise that you are a tornado in power of your thoughts and nobody can suck out the positive vortex from within or add a negative spin to your world.

***Mind Map 2:   Connect with your body, mind and soul.
Take out ten minutes to sit in a quiet place and absorb the events of the day whilst clearing your mind off all the clutter.***

> *Stop ...   and smell the fresh air,*
>
> *Stop ...   and see the world moving,*
>
> *Stop ...   and feel yourself as a part of this world,*
>
> *Stop ...   and understand that your heart beats with your thoughts and feelings.*

Even the brain needs regular spring cleaning of unhealthy negative thoughts. A healthy mind equates a healthy body. Learn to sink the negative thoughts and float the positive ones while you drown the negative memories and rescue the positive memories.

You can achieve this once you understand your own mind and its healing abilities. For this to happen, you must have an insight into your tactile and emotional sensations. Remember that the body is connected to the mind which is connected to a higher energy within called the Soul. Once you are able to establish this connection, the process of healing begins.

By striking a balance within the heart and mind, allows for the soul to reach equilibrium. The journey begins.

You. The Journey Begins

Chapter 2

Your past shapes your future.

Sometimes in life, we get lost along our journey, confused, negative, our mind swaying aimlessly like a helpless boat at the mercy of a stormy ocean. *The sixth golden rule is that you need to still your mind and understand your future goals by remembering your past actions.*

I was a mere five year old little girl who grew up with big dreams within my heart. As I stood in the balcony of our tiny one bedroomed apartment overlooking a luscious green park, my thoughts would wonder into a yonder majestic white mansion. Every year, this luxurious home would be brightly lit during the festival season with a tall snowy tree dazzling with colours of silver, red, yellow, pink and gold. I hailed from a very poor family and let alone a tree, could not even afford dinner on most days which was a simple meal of dry bread and water. As I watched the children from the gigantic house across us dancing around their tree, my eleven little friends from the neighbourhood gaped in awe. Sam, the eldest of our troupe sighed that he wished we had a tree as well to which I responded that if we try, we may achieve. Alvin did not think that we would get a tree and laughed at my earnest thoughts. I then set out to fulfil the dream of my friends against all odds.

I tossed and turned that night as I lay awake thinking of how was I going to pay for such an expensive tree. A thought flickered through my mind. Eureka! If I could not buy a tree, I would have to grow my own but where do I get the money for seeds. I remembered that the kind old lady from the neighbourhood Mrs C. used to grow beautiful daffodils, geraniums and marigolds. Her garden was the fragrance of summer blended with the freshness of spring. I walked up to the door of the old brown house with a red tin roof and knocked with care. Mrs C. opened the creaky huge wooden door. She invited me in as I relayed my request to her. 'Well now young lady,' she smiled through her glowing eyes, 'I will give you some seeds but first you must work for it.' I agreed without a second thought and set out to work in the blazing sun which involved planting pumpkin seeds, sunflower seeds and curry leaves. At the end of two weeks, Mrs C. rewarded my hard work with five large yellowish-brown seeds.

I set out myself to plant the seeds in the park across me. Sam and friends watched me daily as I nurtured the seeds carefully sprinkling water and ensuring the soil was intact. The first few days brought disappointment as the birds had found four seeds and flew off with it. I then realised that maybe they were hungry and then set out to dig a deeper hole and buried the last seed within. One day, my brother came running to call me. He said he had noticed that the seed was sprouting. I jumped for joy and thereafter as the days turned into night, and autumn to spring, we had a tiny tree in the park. By December, every friend in the neighbourhood danced around the tree as we made our own special decorations from tin cans and coloured cardboard paper.

Today, this tree is the largest tree in the neighbourhood and about me, well; I live in that white house now. I was able to do so by remembering where I was in the past and understanding where I wanted to be in the future. This motivates you to build courage and willpower to charge ahead with your goals to shape your destiny. Our roots are very much like the tree whereby we should never forget our foundation. Just remember, your past is what has made 'You' today to become a much more improved 'You' for a better tomorrow. *The seventh golden rule is to draw strength from your positive past experiences.*

Mind Map 3: Answer these three magical questions to help you pave your destiny.

1. Where have I come from?

2. How far have I travelled?

3. Where do I intend going to?

'YOU' are the captain of your own ship and only YOU can navigate your course.

So set sail to your destination and keep the faith for calm seas'.

Chapter 3

Faith and Fate

It was a cold, stormy October afternoon and I was late to board a flight. As I arrived at the boarding gates, the ground stewardess informed me that the boarding gate just closed. I pleaded with her to open the gate as the aeroplane had not as yet departed. She refused quoting the airline policy and then arranged to have me board a later flight. It was my first lesson on fighting destiny. As I sat in the airport lounge, I had received news that the aeroplane which took off had to return to the airport due to a faulty engine.

I then set off to board the later flight onward bound to Durban. My thoughts were still focused on the previous missed flight as I stared into the distant horizon. The plane which I was in, suddenly flew into a thunderstorm at 35 000 feet above sea level. It was the most turbulent flight I had ever experienced. There was pitch blackness within the dark thunderclouds and all that could be seen were flashes of blinding lightning within. We were definitely caught in an electrical thunderstorm. The lightning struck the plane on its right wing, the side which I was sitting at causing the aircraft to tilt and lose control plummeting downwards. Passengers on-board, along with the air hostesses, were terrified and screaming.

I began to pray as I felt that this was the end of the road. What happened next was nothing short of a miracle. I had witnessed the most phenomenal sight in my existence; a bright glowing sun appeared by magic within the darkness. I had my cellular mobile in my hand so quickly captured this one moment in time.

Within minutes, the flight gained control but the bright ball of light had sort of released another tiny glowing ball which began descending. I attempted to analyse this occurrence as a reflection but to my amazement it was not at all because the tiny ball of light travelled with the plane whilst the larger ball of light stayed 'stationary' within its context. It seemed as if the little light had been guiding us and on touchdown, as we disembarked the plane, both lights were fully present in their aura thus dispelling the analysis of a reflection.

You are connected to the Universe which constantly guides 'You'. When an aeroplane taxes at 80km/hr on the runway, its destination lays in the control of the pilot and as the aircraft flies at 360km/hr in the sky, its destiny lays in the hands of the Universe and its Creator.

There are many doors within our lives that are gateways to our destiny. Never fear or fight a closing door. When one door shuts another shall always open. Such is the power of the Universe whereby one can only perceive their future ten years down the line whilst the Universe knows your fate a hundred years in advance.

Certain things are not meant to be for reasons that we cannot foresee. Instead of draining your energies within that which is pointless, redirect your strengths elsewhere which may make a positive difference in your life and thus unlock your potential for a better and brighter future. Keep your faith strong that regardless of the circumstances, what is meant to be will be, and what is not meant to be will set you free.

The only link between what is and what is not; is the Bridge of Faith.

You. The Journey Begins

Chapter 4

Peace is a friendship which begins within you.

Inner-peace is one of the most important aspects of a holistic functioning person and it begins with 'You', the person.

The physical, socio-economic and political variables impact greatly on the healthcare of the individual and its nation. It can have a positive effect or catastrophic effect. The physical factors such as war and disasters cause more mortality and disability than any disease. It not only destroys the external social support environment of the individual but also manifests as physical and psychological trauma to adults and children. Children especially are prone to an endemic poverty, disabilities and malnutrition diseases apart from psychological traumatic stress disorders. This disrupts the peaceful processes of both the internal and external environment.

However, the journey always begins within 'You'. One spends much time fighting with those who do not matter than fighting for those who do matter and thus loses valuable time and precious sleep. You then acquire stress, anger and frustration and upset the peaceful healthy processes of the environment around you. It is important physically, psychologically and spiritually to attain inner peace before this peace is spread throughout because you need to be focused first before undertaking the correct decisions in life which impact not only on you, but others around you. For this to occur, you must begin to set priorities to place yourself first i.e. your health, body and mind must be given attention before you can attempt to assist others. If you are of a sound body and mind, you will be able to create positive peaceful bridges within your family and extended relationships.

Although man (humankind) can control the environment, this very environment also influences man. As mentioned earlier, a person's environment includes many factors namely physical, socio-economic, biological and political. Some of these factors are variables which are either dependent or interdependent upon the person. These environmental factors play either a positive or negative impact on the person and their surroundings and are frequently interconnected. It can either contribute to a peaceful sphere within the person and their surroundings or it can destroy this very sphere, both within and around the individual.

In attaining inner peace, a sense of calmness sets in that as you think, so too shall you become. This allows you to think positively as you have a better focus and understanding of your environment and instead of the environment controlling you, 'You' begin to control the environment.

Someday, just like the flash of a camera, your life will flash before your very eyes. You spend so much time worrying and being anxious than planning on how you are going to live happy. When you go into a supermarket to buy a tub of yoghurt, the first thing you do is to look at the expiry date. You then have to enjoy this delicious yoghurt before the expiry date or it is too late. You are thus caught in this web of deadlines, timeframes and dates pondering over planning for the future.

Unlike the yoghurt, your body does not come with a visible expiry date.

So go out there and enjoy each moment and make it treasurable because why wait for your life to flash before your eyes on the expiry date? What about today? What about now? Let it flash across whilst you are alive so you will be able to accomplish all what you haven't and say the things and do the things which you have always hoped for thus finding that inner-peace within you. 'You' will then realise the controlling factors of deadlines, timeframes and routine and will thus be able to manage this. In attaining this inner-peace, you will be able to stay focused and direct your internal environment. Peace is strength and it begins within you thus you must make peace within yourself.

You. The Journey Begins

Chapter 5

Fear, Failure and Doom; Replace your negative world into a positive life.

It was almost 10 o' clock at night when I received a call from my study partner. We were in our final year of medical studies and the pressure was on to perform at our optimal best to ensure a successful pass rate. Riya was in a state of panic as she screamed out to me that she was experiencing a tight chest and felt dizzy. 'Nirvadha, I need your help, I think I am having a heart attack.' At the sound of these words, I raced over to her apartment and found her hyperventilating. I managed to calm her down and realised that the symptoms she was experiencing seemed similar to a heart attack, but not quite specific. As the last session of my psychiatry lecture stayed fresh within mind, I recalled what my professor had taught me; that an anxiety or panic attack may present with almost similar symptoms as a heart attack.

Your next question would then be what is anxiety and how is it related to 'You'? Well anxiety is simply a medical term used for a disorder which creates fear, worrying, or nervousness. These disorders usually affect how we feel and behave. They can even manifest as real physical symptoms such as chest pains, a pounding heart and dizziness which Riya experienced. Depending on the level of anxiety, it can seriously impact on your daily life activities.

The mind is strongly linked to the physical body and what we experience within the mind usually manifests as physical symptoms. We all undergo a general state of worry or fear before confronting something challenging such as a school test, university examination or job interview and this is normal. However these symptoms interfere with a person's ability to sleep or their daily activities if it is not controlled.

Many factors can trigger fear such as abuse or the loss of a loved one however stress contributes to a major role in fear and anxiety. Students at school may become stressed during examinations which will impact negatively in their social and family lives. Stress manifests even in personal relationships where partners experience constant fighting and huge relationship differences.

Anxiety is also associated with medical conditions such as asthma and several heart conditions. One may become stressed if diagnosed with a terminal illness. The side effects of certain medication may even contribute to anxiety. Intoxication from alcohol or an illicit drug, such as cocaine, can cause anxiety. Withdrawal from an illicit drug, such as heroin, or from prescription drugs may also cause anxiety.

Most healthcare professionals can diagnose anxiety. If you are consulting your physician for anxiety or symptoms related to this, the physician will take a careful medical and personal history from you. Be sure to disclose all life events and any medication you are taking to your physician. A physical examination will be undertaken by your physician who will then order laboratory tests to exclude any medical illnesses causing the anxiety.

You must also learn to manage the stressors in your life. Manage your timeframes and work deadlines to free you for some 'me-time'. There are many relaxation techniques such as meditation and yoga which you may incorporate into your daily life. Make a list of the negative thoughts you have and write a list of positive thoughts to replace them. It is therapeutic to talk about your fears to a confidante as this helps alleviate stress.

Exercise is very important in distracting the mind from negative thoughts. It allows fresh oxygen to enter the lungs and fresh positive thoughts to penetrate the mind. If you are hyperventilating, always keep a paper bag near you and breathe in and out into the bag until your lungs have reached an equilibrium where you are able to breathe normally once again. Should you find the tension building up within 'You', take a long walk or drive as time usually heals and dissipates the steaming vapour of anger.

You are what you eat so reduce your intake of caffeine, coffee or tea and chocolate consumption which does impact on your mental being aggravating the stress. Inform your physician if you are using over-the-counter remedies or herbal remedies to see if they contain chemicals that may contribute to anxiety. Certain weight loss herbal remedies contain excess caffeine and other stimulants which may exacerbate anxiety. Refrain from alcohol and stop any illicit substance abuse.

Once again, it must be reinforced as mentioned earlier, that the brain always needs regular spring cleaning of unhealthy thoughts. Drown those negative thoughts and filter only positive thoughts to float the surface. Always face every situation in a positive manner. Challenges exist to be solved and if all were known to the world, our lives would be boring. There is strength in fear of the unknown, the strength to find solutions, untap your problem solving potential and thus develop your mind to greater levels and become a stronger 'You'.

Never be afraid of what you fear because in this very fear lies your strength to embrace the unknown to become known so that you face it positively.

Chapter 6

Believe in 'You'.

It was my first day of work as an intern doctor at a hospital in Durban a few years ago. As I passed the female medical ward, I heard the sobbing of a teenaged female patient. On entering the room, I saw Amara crying endlessly in her pillow. I went on to ask her, 'What seems to be the problem my dear?' 'She responded that 'Dreams do not come true.' I then held her hand and told her a little story of my own.

When the Wright brothers looked up into sky, people laughed at them saying that humans would never fly; today we have aeroplanes. When Niel Armstrong looked up at the moon, people jested that humans would never fly into space; he was the first man to giant step the moon. When Alexander Graham Bell invented the photophone, people prodded at him; yet today we have mobile phones with internet. When Thomas Edison told the world that his electric bulb will replace the candle, people teased that he was still in the dark ages; yet he had brought light to the world.

She then replied, 'Doc, that was all a part of history and I will never be a great as them.' My response to her was, 'You are great in your own way. Dreams do come true if you have a vision. When I was a little girl, I always dreamed to be either a doctor or a ballerina. One of those choices came true.' She then exclaimed that she too wished to be a doctor someday. So my little friend hugged me and said that she will be positive. And guess what? She is currently an aspiring medical student at one of our universities.

The greatest innate acquisition of a human is the ability to weave dreams and aspirations. Far greater than this is the actual ability to reach out to your dream and draw it to reality. However many people fail to accomplish this task due to a simple barrier; the lack of willpower. 'You' within must learn to tap into that willpower and gain the confidence to believe in yourself. If you cannot have faith in yourself, do not expect others to have faith in you. It begins within 'You'.

Go ahead and write out your dreams. Write it on a piece of paper and let the energies of your body flow into the ink and engrave your emotions onto the paper. You now have your actual feelings on paper however, what should the next step be? You need to identify key people, key organisations or even qualities within yourself which will assist in your venture. Never be afraid to ask for advice because there is a high chance that somebody will assist you in the appropriate direction. If you do not convert your thought into an action, it will always remain a thought and years into the future it would be too late for the famous question, what if? 'You' and only you have the power to unleash your dreams.

Nobody knew that Sherpa Tenzing would be one of the individuals to reach the summit of Mount Everest, but he climbed his way to success, and you can do this too.

Remember that once you believe, you achieve.

You. The Journey Begins

Chapter 7

The Healing Power of Love.

Winter leaves falling down,
As snow begins to melt,
Ice cold wind cuts through me,
Just as how your heart had felt.
As day turns to night, night turns to day,
Spring arrives with her healing balm,
Flowers bloom with a fragrance so sweet,
Your heart begins to finally warm.

The greatest philosophers have tried to define love. The truth is that love cannot be defined, it can only be felt. It is said that if you love something set it free, if it comes back it is yours and if it does not, it never was. Indeed another deceiving thought because love is not meant to be caged but rather it is born to be lived. When we begin to possess and obsess over certain virtues and emotions, we begin to lose focus of our path. The inner 'You' becomes uncontrollable resulting in mood swings and depression. You must first understand the several concepts of 'You' and one of these concepts is that the 'You' loves to flow with emotions and not be restrained.

Have you ever noticed a beautiful white dove fly? Can you imagine this dove being in a cage? It will barely be able to move and constantly fight against all barriers to leave the cage thus utilising its entire energy to be set free. The human mind is similar whereby when you cage a thought or emotion, the mind becomes restless and wants to be freed. In doing so, your body takes a toll by paying in valuable energy that is misdirected.

Love is an abstract emotion which triggers powerful happy hormones within your immune system causing you to heal. At times with the emotions of love, we laugh, cry, jump, fly and even go crazy. However the most beautiful gift which our Creator has bestowed upon us, is the ability to love as a human being. Love invokes a diverse colourful canvas of emotions including happiness, sadness, joy, pain, passion and creativity. These are the very emotions which add an exciting dimension to life hence I believe that love is life.

The most important concept of love begins with loving yourself. If you cannot love or even respect yourself, then do not expect another to reciprocate this. When you begin to love yourself, 'You' then begin to understand the core essence of love. 'You' then identify with the concepts of trust, respect, honesty and truth which ultimately results in valuing yourself. Once you begin to treasure yourself, your focus begins to magnify and you become rooted in your confidence. Your judgement is clearer and you become resolute in decision-making as your confidence is unwavering. Why wait, start loving yourself today and treasure the importance of 'You' within the vast Universe.

Love is a healing power which begins within 'You'.

You. The Journey Begins

Chapter 8

You are your own competition.

Many of you would have made resolutions to aim for success. Attaining this success always comes at a price of working both hard and smart depending on what your real goals are.

Sometimes, you may work both hard and smart, but feel that you have failed. This was the case of my two friends, Candice and Kayla, who were both very dedicated towards their aim which was winning a beauty pageant in their hometown. The two beautiful girls worked tirelessly at the gym for many hours and studied all the general knowledge questions of the world. On the day of the contest, sadly only one could be crowned as the Queen. Kayla, who didn't make the top three placements, sank into a major depression thinking she had disappointed her family miserably.

Her mother called me up a few days before her birthday and said that Kayla was admitted into one of the local hospitals from a drug overdose. I went to visit her and was deeply concerned by the deteriorated state of her health. I quickly arranged a counsellor and psychologist to assess her. Her mother played the self-blame saying that it was her fault to push her daughter too far to win this contest. I consoled them by adding that the entire family, friends and healthcare practitioners supporting Kayla must be very positive in order to help her break the barrier of depression. Today, I am proud to say that Kayla is happily married and is a fashion designer entrepreneur.

On meeting her a few months ago, she said she couldn't believe that she was the same person obsessively driven to determination. I then informed her that there are many objectives in life, but just one goal. Regardless of the many objectives you do not attain, you still must stay in sight of your goal, the one which will bring you real success ultimately. Remember that there is no such thing as failure. If you didn't attain one of your objectives, either you try again or realise that it may not be meant for you whilst there are other greater objectives destiny has awaiting you.

As for beauty pageants and other talent contests, there are sets of criteria set by those particular organisations which many individuals do not meet. It does not mean you are any less beautiful or talented. It means that if you were not selected, you must rise above all these competitions and compete with yourself and attain higher goals. You are special and since inner beauty cannot be measured, you are beyond any competition.

Stay focused on the goal in your sight and your sight on

your goal.
Never be distracted and keep firmly rooted.

Success shall then be yours.

You. The Journey Begins

Chapter 9

Be Yourself.

As first year students many years ago, we were still trying to find ourselves within society. I was one of three friends who always wrote my college lecture notes in the manner I understood it. Leyla, who was the tiny and timid one, felt it smarter to leave a dictaphone next to the lecturer so she could have word for word copied into her notes. Pam, who was the brave and outspoken one, felt it best to get the lecturer's slides directly from him. It was a few days before our mid-year examinations when I met my friends for a quick cup of coffee at the student's cafeteria. Pam and Leyla scoffed at the idea of writing lecture notes as it was so time consuming and out dated. Furthermore, my notes were always written using colourful pens and they felt it was a waste.

As our conversation centred on the paper, a few more students entered the chat. They too felt that it was a complete waste to write notes and only nerds did it. I maintained a level head though feeling a bit disappointed that I was being made to be a foolish and not-so-cool student. I mean the very mention of the word 'nerd' brought to mind huge black spectacles and oily gelled hair which certainly was not me, not that I had a problem with anybody who manifested that particular appearance.

The examination was over that winter and time for our results. I stood in line moving closer to the examination notice board and then saw the disappointed look in many faces. Almost half the class had failed, including Leyla and Pam. I had passed but didn't really wish to inform the others since I felt their pain as well. However, Pam knew my examination number and shouted out to the others that I had passed.

The lecturer walked by and everybody stopped him to enquire from him as to why they had failed. He informed them that although they had taken the notes from him word for word, the important part of the examination was not in regurgitating the work but in applying the theories. He then smiled at me and said that the use of colours for mind mapping was important in being able to relate the information back onto paper as it demonstrated an understanding of several concepts. Since that day, Pam and Leyla along with the others went out to buy colourful gel pens and begun making their own notes. Well as for me, I became the scribe writer at times for the slow coaches who could not keep up to speed with the lecturer. This was my first lesson at college which had taught me to be myself.

Summer begun to take shape and we were invited to Pam's twenty first birthday party. I recall the exquisite red, gold and black satin, silk and lace fabrics waltzing into the lounge area. Here I was in this plain and simple beige frock draped in a brown shawl to hide a discoloured fabric stain, feeling so underdressed. Everybody asked each other, "Who are you wearing?" Several top designer names were thrown into the air when the question was asked to me. I softly whispered, "I am wearing myself". There were a few chuckles but I felt a level of confidence that I am me, and people have to love the inner me.

As Pam walked onto the stage, her heel caught in the step and as she fell, a strip of the red shoulder strap tore. Whilst some were laughing at her, I walked forward, picked her up from the floor and wrapped my shawl around her. Her family just walked into the hall and thanked me. The proudest moment was when Pam called her best friend to deliver a speech. That person was me. I walked onto the platform and spoke from my heart receiving a standing ovation from my peers. The second lesson for that year was in never fearing the original 'You' within which was me.

"You do not need a spotlight to be in the limelight, you are your own light."

"Define yourself within your own existence."

"Your Soul is original so become your own creation."

You. The Journey Begins

Chapter 10

'You' are your greatest source of inspiration

Life is like a garden of memories which is either nurtured with a sprinkle of positivity or destroyed by a thunderstorm of negativity.

We always feel doomed when faced with difficult challenges. The fact is that challenges exist for you to solve them and triumph. Always face each challenge in a positive manner and only then will you be able to view the winning post. The minute you allow a negative thought to enter your mind, you begin to sink with the negative dead wood and thus struggle to swim out of a muddy sinkhole of negativity.

Steady the mind and keep calm.

Self-reflect and absorb your thoughts for the day. Try and understand difficulties from different perspectives.

View all challenges as if they are not your own and then provide the advice.

Think out of the box.

Walk ten steps in front of your problem, two steps around and one step behind so you have covered all angles.

Just as how every beautiful flower has to outgrow its thorns to bloom, so too do you have to weather all criticisms prior to success and victory. Embrace the positive criticisms and self-reflect upon this to uplift your character. Repel the negative criticisms as this does not reflect your character, it reflects only the darkness within that source.

Keep moving to the light never swaying from your destined path.

"We always see the beauty of the sunflower but never imagine the power of its seed."

"Grow your mind and bloom beyond all fields."

Yes, awaken yourself, awaken your existence.

BL100812-145
BluLotis Self Publishing Services

9 780620 716215

www.ingramcontent.com/pod-product-compliance
Lightning Source LLC
Chambersburg PA
CBHW020023050426
42450CB00005B/618